AF599278

GREAT SPORTS RIVALRIES

BAYERN MUNICH

Jamie Fickett

REAL MADRID

A Stingray Book
SEAHORSE PUBLISHING

Teaching Tips for Caregivers and Teachers:

This Hi-Lo book features high-interest subject matter that will appeal to all readers in intermediate and middle school grades. It may be enjoyed by students reading at or above grade level as well as by those who are looking for age-appropriate themes matched with a less challenging reading level. Hi-Lo books are ideal for ELL readers, too.

Each book appeals to a striving reader's age and maturity level. Opportunities are provided for students to read words they already know while encountering a limited number of new, high-interest vocabulary words. With these supports in place, students will read more fluently while increasing reading comprehension. Use the following suggestions to help students grow as readers.

- Encourage the student to read independently at home.
- Encourage the student to practice reading aloud.
- Encourage activities that require reading.
- Establish a regular reading time.
- Have the student write questions about what they read.

Teaching Tips for Teachers:

Before Reading

- Ask, "What do I know about this topic?"
- Ask, "What do I want to learn about this topic?"

During Reading

- Ask, "What is the author trying to teach me?"
- Ask, "How is this like something I already know?"

After Reading

- Discuss how the text features (headings, index, etc.) help with understanding the topic.
- Ask, "What interesting or fun fact did you learn?"

TABLE OF CONTENTS

POWER ON THE PITCH

FC Bayern Munich and Real Madrid CF are teams that often qualify to play in the Union of European Football Associations (UEFA) Champions League.

Some of the best soccer players in the world have played for these teams. Matchups are always exciting.

But the clubs don't like each other very much. Their **rivalry** is one of the most intense in all of sports.

FUN FACT

The city of Madrid is in the country of Spain. The city of Munich is in the country of Germany. Both are on the continent of Europe.

Plus500
Trade Online
10
adidas

1976: THE BEGINNING

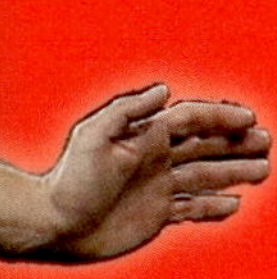

Madrid and Munich have played each other in the Champions League at least 26 times.

Of those matches, Real won 12 and Bayern won 11. Three were ties. Real scored 41 goals to Bayern's 39.

The first matchup was in 1976. Munich won 3 to 1 on **aggregate** over Madrid in the **semifinals**.

FUN FACT

Under Champions League rules, teams play two matches, or legs, before one team advances to the next round. A team's aggregate score combines points from both legs.

1986: AN EARLY LEAD

The rivals faced off in the 1986 semifinals.

Led by a great performance from Lothar Matthäus, Bayern won the first leg 4 to 1. They scored all four goals before the 60-minute mark.

Real won the second leg 1 to 0. However, the aggregate score moved Bayern on to the final.

FUN FACT

Lothar Matthäus holds the record for playing in five consecutive World Cups.

Lothar Matthäus

1999: SPANISH SURPRISE

Nicolas Anelka

Real was the **underdog** in the 1999 semifinal against Bayern. Fans hoped that new player Nicolas Anelka would be a star. But he had not scored yet in the Champions League.

Then, in minute four of the first leg, Anelka sprang into action. He kicked the ball over the outstretched arms of star Bayern goalkeeper Oliver Kahn.

Anelka scored again in the second leg. Madrid advanced to the final.

FUN FACT

The Madrid nickname* Los Blancos *means "whites." That's because the team always wears white uniforms when they play at home.

2000: LONG SHOT

Madrid dominated most of the first leg match in the 2000 semifinals against Bayern.

But in minute 55, Giovane Elber's left foot found the ball in the air. He was 30 yards (27 meters) away from the goal. His kick launched the ball right over Iker Casillas, the star Real goalie who had fallen to the ground.

Bayern won the match 1 to 0.

FUN FACT

***Bayern** is the German name for the state of Bavaria. Munich is the state's capital city.*

Iker Casillas

2003: A BRAWL

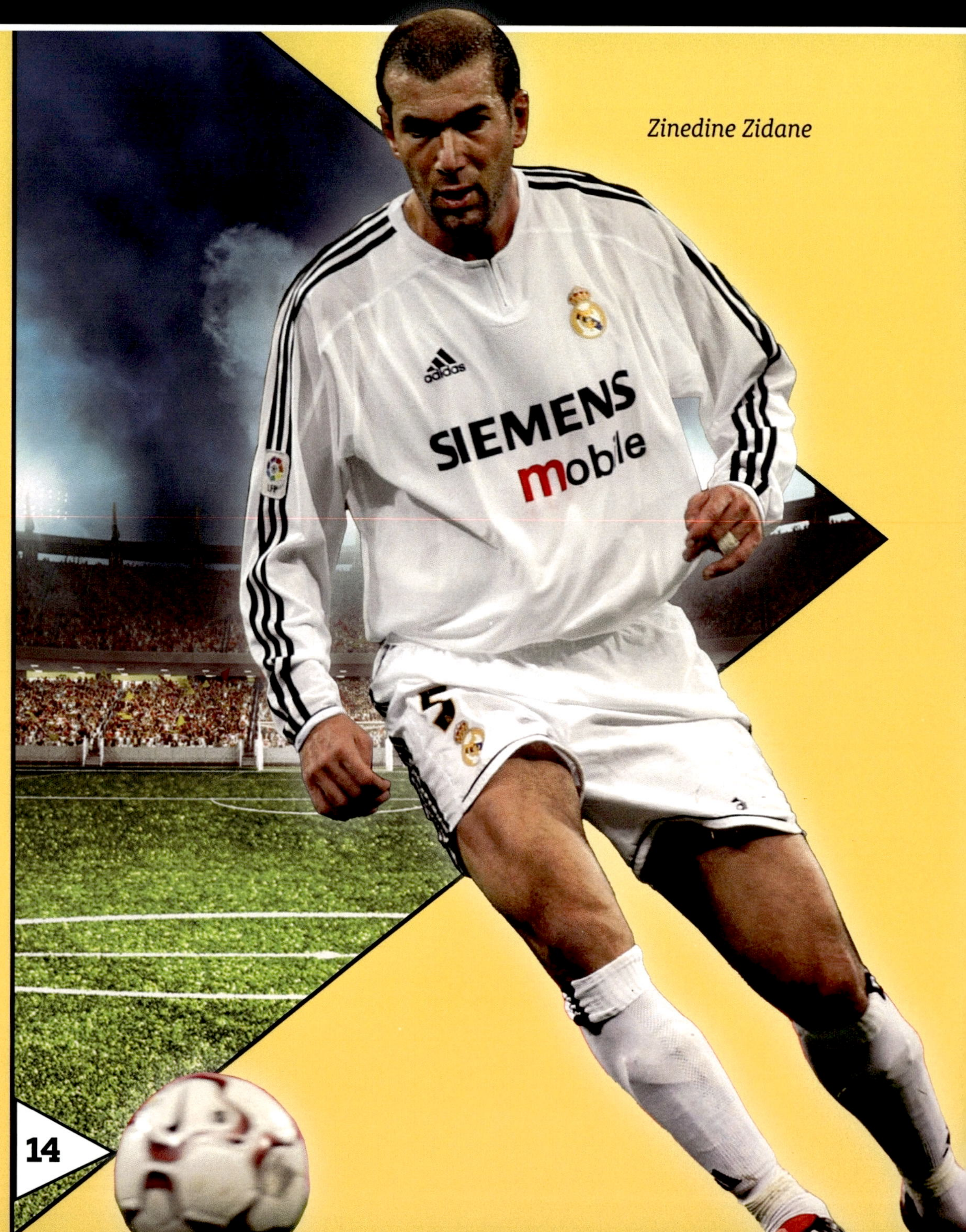

Zinedine Zidane

Legend Zinedine Zidane was at the end of his career in 2003. But he helped Madrid advance to the **quarterfinals** with a win over Bayern.

After a pass by teammate David Beckham, Zidane sent the ball into the goal with a karate-style kick.

The match ended with a **brawl**. It started with yelling and shoving by Real player Guti and Bayern player Bixente Lizarazu.

2011: SHOOTOUT

The two clubs faced off in the 2011 semifinals.

Bayern won the first leg 2 to 1 with a goal by **striker** Mario Gómez. In the second leg, star player Cristiano Ronaldo scored two goals for Real. Madrid won it 2 to 1.

But the aggregate score was tied. A **penalty shootout** would decide the semifinal winner. The Madrid kickers were no match for Bayern goalie Manuel Neuer. Munich won 3 to 1 on penalties.

FUN FACT

Ronaldo has the most international goals of any active male player.

Manuel Neuer

2017: REPEAT FOR REAL

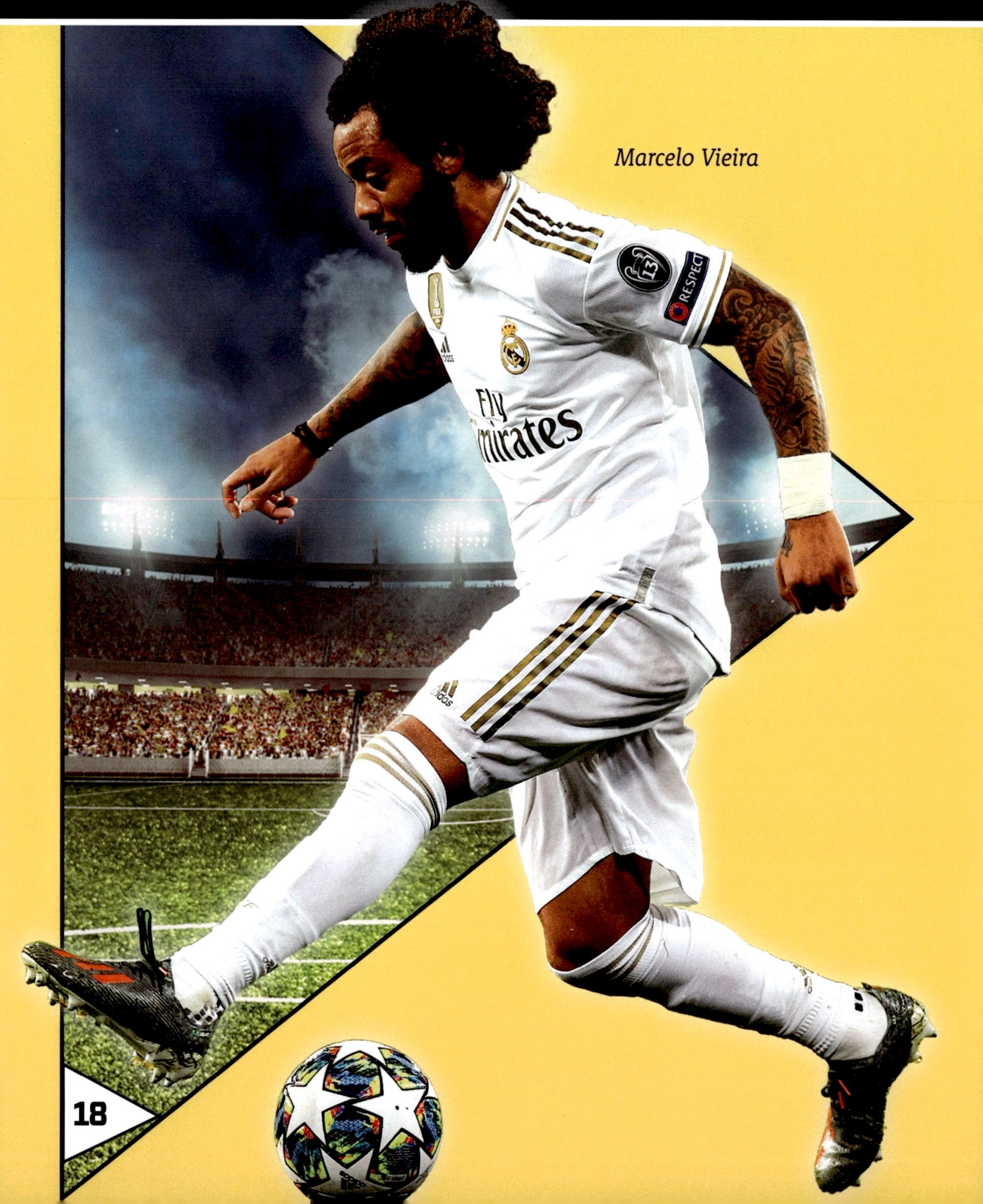

Marcelo Vieira

Madrid wanted to knock Bayern out of the competition in 2017, just like they had the year before.

Real won the first leg semifinal match 2 to 1. Marcelo Vieira and Marco Asensio scored for Madrid. The second leg ended in a 2 to 2 tie. Joshua Kimmich and James Rodríguez scored for Bayern.

Real won with an aggregate score of 4 to 3. They went on to win the final for the third year in a row.

FUN FACT

Team captain Marcelo has won 25 trophies. He is the most decorated player in the history of Real Madrid.

THE RIVALRY CONTINUES

Today's star players continue the **epic** rivalry between Bayern Munich and Real Madrid.

Real forward Vinícius Júnior plays against Bayern's star defense led by Matthijs de Ligt and Alphonso Davies.

Who will win the next battle between these two great teams?

Vinícius Júnior

Alphonso Davies

GLOSSARY

aggregate (AG-ri-git): the combined number of goals scored by two teams over two or more games

brawl (brawl): a rough or noisy fight

epic (EP-ik): amazing or impressive

penalty shootout (PEN-uhl-tee SHOOT-out): in tournament play, a tie-breaking method in which five players from each team take shots on goal until one team comes out ahead

quarterfinals (KWOR-tur-fye-nuhls): in a tournament, the round of play before the semifinals; in the Champions League, eight teams compete in the quarterfinals

rivalry (RYE-vuhl-ree): a longstanding, competitive, up-and-down relationship between two teams

semifinals (SEM-ee-fye-nuhls): in a tournament, the round of play before the final game; in the Champions League, four teams play in the semifinals

striker (STRI-kuhr): a player whose job is to make shots on goal and score points

underdog (UHN-dur-dawg): the team that is expected to lose a match

INDEX

AFTER READING QUESTIONS

1. Which team has won more matches against the other in the Champions League?
2. Who won the 2011 semifinals? How?
3. Why is Cristiano Ronaldo a star player?
4. How long did it take Bayern to score four goals in the 1986 semifinals?
5. Who is Madrid's current star forward?

ABOUT THE AUTHOR

Jamie Fickett lives in Long Island, New York. He enjoys sports, especially baseball. He likes to go to Mets games to watch his favorite player, Pete Alonso, play. He also enjoys cooking his famous chili and watching Formula 1 racing.

Written by: Jamie Fickett
Design by: Kathy Walsh
Editor: Kim Thompson

Photographs/Shutterstock/Newscom: Cover: Oscar J Barroso/LPS via ZUMA Press, Jorge Gonzalez Moreno; p 5, 6, 9, 10, 13, 14, 17, 18, 21: alphaspirit.it; p 5: Juanjo Martin; p 6: FMB/WENN.com/viaNewscom; p 9: Luigi Rizzo; p 10: John Dawes; p 13: F√É¬°Bio Po√É¬ßO; p 14: Robin Nordlund; p 17: Juan Soliz, PacificCoastNews; p 18: Legan P. Mace/ SOPA Images; p 20: Anthony Oliveira; p 21: Frank Hoermann/SVEN SIMON

Library of Congress PCN Data
Bayern Munich vs. Real Madrid /Jamie Fickett
Great Sports Rivalries
ISBN 979-8-8873-5948-9 (hard cover)
ISBN 979-8-8873-5987-8 (paperback)
ISBN 979-8-8904-2046-6 (EPUB)
ISBN 979-8-8904-2105-0 (eBook)
Library of Congress Control Number: 2023912488

Printed in the United States of America.

Seahorse Publishing Company
www.seahorsepub.com

Published in the United States
Seahorse Publishing
PO Box 771325
Coral Springs, FL 33077